Wolf Girls

vs.

Horse Girls

Game Over Books
www.gameoverbooks.com

TABLE OF CONTENTS

& after

WHY I DON'T EAT FRUIT

yesterday my therapist said   i think you may have been molested
     and too young to remember it
she said   there are usually   clues

i don't know
much about dream interpretation but i'm suspicious
of how often sex makes me disappear

re: the orange or the plum   the questioning comes
as it always does
don't you want to taste it   but these ones are special   just try some

or if you nod and say   so it's a texture thing then
i will probably say   probably
but i will be thinking of

          the texture of porcelain
          the texture of wet skin
          the texture of all the times i have vanished

into rot and shame
you can call it a phobia if that helps you put down the knife
but it's more like   a distrust

          of poisoning
contamination from the inside to the outside
to the hands

to the mouth under the tongue
membranes   between the teeth
sticky on the chin   i will not

touch a picture of a pear in a book or hold
a can of peaches in the store   i want
safe clothes in case i need to run   i am

looking for the exit door
in case a place to go is required   there is
lingering damage and   i can't

explain all of it   can you picture me as a piece
of clothing on the floor   can you picture me as a new
moon hiding its face   can you picture a silent

child becoming all this
          or anybody
                    else

girl

I CAN GUESS WHAT INSTRUMENT YOU PLAYED IN MIDDLE SCHOOL BAND

but what I mean is did anybody ever call you queer during inside recess when the rain fell too thick to spill us outside like a split bag of sugar so instead we played hangman on the whiteboard & made cruel games of MASH & called me queer in our most indoor of voices & how was it that October wrapped oak roots around our ankles & we looked ahead to all that might come of a sleepover that didn't & of the Book Fair that did & once someone wore a toga to the dance & how everyone laughed because courage looks funny before we ever really had to be brave & I feel like I knew you then even though I didn't & I bet you wanted to play the saxophone but got told the clarinet was easier & now you don't play anything except spotify & saxophone regret sits briefly on your tongue like a dry reed but then melts like words chalked out before a storm

WHY AM I LIKE THIS

in 7th grade I was sure my crush would love me
if we wore the same size shoes
so I convinced my parents to buy me sneakers to grow on
this was my Very Good Plan for getting a boyfriend

at the pool party I tried to demonstrate I was ready to be asked out
      look! we both wear size 9 ha ha
he glanced at my feet and said
               yours are women's not men's
                    we still wear different sizes

I tell this story like it's funny because dramatic irony
is when the audience knows something the characters don't

by 8th grade I hoped if I called the pretty ones boring
enough times I might steal all their boyfriends
tell me, if life isn't a competition
why am I trying so hard to win it

one time I ran the mile in gym
& my face stayed red for hours
one time I flashed some grownups
just trying to have a quiet lunch
one time I emailed my friend from a fake hotmail to say
nobody likes you because you're a bitch

I explain all this to help you understand why I resented the Spice Girls
there were so many   and none of them were me

SORRY DAY

The chat service AOL Instant Messenger was permanently shut down on December 15, 2017.

I proclaim, one day each year, we find each other in the Database of Screennames
and apologize for the easy cruelties we enacted without knowing that the pain
we cause still counts as pain. Make it a bank holiday. Make it a festival
of door-opening sound effects; make us feel the exhilaration of somebody
we ache to talk to finally logging on. The remembrances will be sweet and silty,
grit in the back of the mouth, sugar on the tongue; granulated nostalgia and regret.
Let us acknowledge our interpersonal lows, like the time I made a burner account
to check if my crush had blocked me because he was tired of talking, and he had.
Let our old internet boyfriends reach beyond their kids and drinking problems
and let them be sorry—not sorry they met us but that they weren't kinder
to the interchangeable girls behind wolffox and penguinsfly and happykitty86—
how disposable I must have seemed to them, a receptacle, a shapeshifting blank.
I still think about the photo of the pretty girl I sent off once, pretending she was me,
a tan leg draped over the monkey bars, freckled and smiling in magazine perfection.
He said: I know this isn't what you look like. He said: lol you don't fool me.
Give me a day for all the times I demanded to be loved by the world,
and wasn't. A day for all the knots we've had to unwind, and the compulsions, too,
the countless ways we still ask the wrong people: am I good enough for you?

13

PRAYER OF THE PORNO TAPE AT THE 8TH GRADE SLEEPOVER

o somebody's older brother
coming in clutch.

praise the ingenuity—
procurement

& concealment.
praise this technology

of recordable VHS,
the forethought of volume

turned all the way
down.

praise parents
who remain

in the kitchen,
unaware of the muted moans.

o mouths! o boobs!
praise your girlness

thrust into
a roomful of boyness.

& blessed be the choice
you make early

to sit behind the tv,
so you can't see the screen,

or rather,
be seen seeing.

you are no coward.
you are a student.

you watch their faces
watch the bodies—

careful masks
in reverent light.

BEFORE THE HARVEST

my body didn't grow up in a vacuum.
it happened unattended in Mr. Cole's homeroom,
with wind sprints and jock jams, at February breakfasts,
my naked feet laid like paper over tepid blowing air.

we were unattended in Mr. Cole's homeroom when
a boy asked how much all the girls weighed,
and my feet laid naked like paper over tepid blowing air.
I was wearing my navy blue shirt with the silver zipper.

a boy asked how much, and all the girls weighed
in. at the full-length mirror in my parent's room
wearing my navy blue shirt with the silver zipper,
fat now congealing into a thing named breasts.

at the full-length mirror in my parent's room,
I planted my thumbnail in soft belly, dug hard into
fat. now congealing into a named thing,
or maybe I just started coming when you called.

so I planted thumbnails, dug hard into
wind sprints and jock jams. grew a February hunger.
or maybe I just started coming when you called
my body   [   ]

SEED BEADS

the best necklace I ever made I wore only to school

dances this was a rule about clothing and special occasions

I kept the string snug against my throat deluxe clasp

at the back twisted shut beads like precious nips

of aurora borealis of course no one knew it was good

but me sometimes it's like I have one eye that goes

all the way through I still feel most hope assembling

oil-slick shards alone on the floor of a half-dark room

WOLF GIRLS

Wolf Girls know facts about wolves
Wolf Girls all have at least 3 wolf books
Wolf Girls draw
alone in their rooms
the animal is not named
but defined by
appointments and diagnoses

                    Wolf Girls with something to prove
                          have mood disorders now
                                  did you know
                    Horse Girls can become Wolf Girls
                                  Horse Girls push
                        the angry chaos in tidy rows
                          a Horse Girl is never
                                  late for supper
                        how could someone dis-
                    appear in all this silver light
                              when did we stop
          telling stories in which we were still wild

VS. HORSE GIRLS

Horse Girls know how to take care of horses
Horse Girls take horse lessons
Horse Girls draw
perfect families holding hands
Bella, Scout, Ransom
obedience of the backbone
work hard

Horse Girls   seems like all of us
want to know how high we can jump
after dark
when the moon is full
Wolf Girls pause
outside their warm homes
unready to enter a well-lit life
a Wolf Girl tucks down a howl
like a dime lost in a coat pocket
show me who you really are
Wolf Girls
lined up for coffee at the drive-thru

WE WERE HIGH UP, MAYBE CROSSING A RIVER

I was sitting in the back of the family
    car, my mom and dad up front.

we were laughing and I remember this
    part very clearly: it was exciting

to spend whole minutes together,
    for once a unit one could stand

roadside and point a finger at going by. look at that
    family. I wonder where they're off to.

I cracked a joke and when it landed,
    my parents' laughter rose a sunburst

in my belly. they were laughing like
    they meant it, the way you would

laugh at something actually funny,
    like at the movies or a new george carlin tape.

unlike how you'd laugh at a kid joke.
    what'd I say? what'd I say?

what's so funny? what's so funny?
    I was greedy to hear

my cleverness retumbled
    off of grownup tongues. to linger there

one moment longer. I must've pushed too far,
    asked in that childish way

to be admired even when you are stupid.
    you know what you said.

I don't remember who said it.
        my father said it. my mother watched

the yellow lines become dots
        become lines become dots.

AMAGANSETT

do you remember
the uncanny thrill
of being ten
and choosing
a breakfast cereal
after waking up
in a not-quite
stranger's house?
their selection baffling–
cereals you'd never
heard of from brands
you suspected
must be years
discontinued
or only available
to purchase in finland
or perhaps popular
in whatever dimension
spawns extended
family with whom
one is not particularly
close.
in the years before
we fractured like sunlight
spilt across the red tile
floor of a summertime
kitchen, we would
migrate from time to time
in volvo station wagons
as was our custom
to a particular house
on the south fork
where my grandfather
was first a boy
and later himself.

it was a whaler's house–
the kind of old place
with surplus rooms
named parlor
and library,
compelling
our hushed reverence
even when
we crept inside
unsupervised
to cascade dominos
onto hooked
judgmental rugs
or to perch on
the full-grain wingback
I would not
have dared to touch
in the witness
of my forebears.
better trafficked
but more puzzling
was the living room
we called new,
which for some
inscrutable
architectural purpose
was encircled
by a shallow trench
between floor and walls–
an indoor moat
filled with pebbles
and dead spiders
crisping
like the elm leaves
that had somehow
infiltrated even down
to the wine cellar.

have you ever
smelled a homestead
unfurling
in an august lull?
some houses
are more interested
in mysteries than comforts.
I imagine this one
like a child picking clothes-
reveling in
its secret reasons
for rain boots
with tutus and purple
pink stripy pajamas.
I prefer
to think with reverence
of the house
as a kindergartener
or an estate which somehow
birthed my mother
or a failed lesson
in which I always
burn the soles
of my bare feet
on the bluestone terrace
and never learn I have to
wear my fucking shoes
when it's sunny,
or a cathedral
or a storybook
or a dream
or a feast
or a myth
than to remember
who was there
and should've loved me
but didn't.

24

TENNIS LESSONS IN ELLSWORTH, MAINE, 1999

there are two courts. I prefer playing by
the door and this lonely section of bleachers.
a singular bleach. the far court feels a bit like

playing tennis on the moon. a lobbed ball arcs slow
because we pay it attention. my serve used to be gentle.
a timid flail of limbs and loosely understood effort.

but then, repetition. the satisfaction
of a physical epiphany. new precision:
shoulder dip, elbow ebb, wrist flex. executing

this sharp dance. now I only hit an easy
serve when I mean for you to send it back.
I learn to move my feet, bend my knees,

get under the ball. I work for every good hustle
from my coach. I am anxious about everything,
all the time, except for in this big, cold room.

even the gear is comforting. contraptions to pick up balls.
contraptions to bat 'em around. I understand my girlness
in relation to who I can out-perform: sometimes I play

one of the boys and I win. but sometimes I have to
play Nicky, who is so hopeless that if I choke, Owen and Jon
laugh about it in the carpool, the whole ride home.

FOR THE BOY WHO MIGHT
HAVE LOVED THE GHOST OF ME

my first god was Mrs. Martin. I prayed
her seating chart would place me by my crush
& almost every month—glory!—in her hands
this miracle would occur. she understood heaven.
in fifth grade, there were so many ways to drown.
lust & love drawn in on the same haunted

tide. I would sometimes fantasize about haunting
him. to literally die & become a ghost. I remember praying
I'd get sick & die or fall down & die or drown
& then I'd return to visit my now-very-sorry crush,
surprise him on the walk home from the bus. heaven
is being desirable, just once to have the upper hand.

one whole afternoon we spent touching hands
when Mrs. Martin assigned us to square dance. haunting
memories dressed up in pit-sweat stained baggy tees—heaven
is do-si-do-ing without having to admit you're into it. I don't pray
out loud, though I always seem to get what I wish for. my crush
grabbed my child tits three years later. drowning

only took a squeeze. one way to kill desire is to drown
it. we grant boys our love & also clever hands.
but I'd already grown up enough to be crushed,
already become a roadside thing, a haunted pelt,
the dullest quillbag, ponytail prey
on a tarnished bed, sourest of heavens.

I made my second god a sensation like heaven,
encouraging every disappointed love to drown
in the next fixation, whatever happens when a prayer
meets sweat. a wrist, a knee, dimple, hand,
brow, temple. I have always been a little haunted
by the effort to seduce myself in the name of a crush.

at the pool party, I remember we drank cokes, crushed
the cans with airwalks & pencil tips. in actual heaven
maybe you wouldn't have to die first to haunt
a boy or two. in my honey tea-steeped dream, I drown
them all & wake up forgiving everybody's hands.
I don't need a new god. just periodic shallow floods. I pray

fondly to the landscape of a finished crush. a drowned heaven,
easy-swaying seaweed trees & mute crab-handed men. haunted
bubbles drifting skyward, tiny breaths of prayer.

NONBINOSAURUS REX

1

in 1869, edward cope discovered the elasmosaurus
but in his haste to publish before his rival
cope reassembled the aquatic dinosaur back to front
head attached to the tail instead of the neck
a blueprint scrambled in the confusion of passing millennia

2

when I was a girl I assumed I would grow up
to be a paleontologist mostly because I wasn't aware
of all the other options
or how it would eventually feel
to dig and dig and dig
only to uncover something obsolete
some stone formed body
a few pressure-crushed fragments
destined to be cobbled together
into a guesswork construct
just so mankind can pretend
they've found the whole monster
earned the right to name it

3

my fifth grade crush asked me out
by leaving a clammy-palmed message
on our family answering machine
I refused to call him back
even though 110% of what I wanted out of life at the time
was to be publicly adored by this specific boy
instead I practiced the piano melodramatically
one-half of a wistful duet until bedtime

4

I feel a bit like the elasmosaurus
like maybe I got myself largely correct
but also fundamentally backwards

5

when I was a girl I assumed I would grow up
to be a woman mostly because I wasn't aware
of all the other options
or how it would eventually feel
to dig and dig and dig
only to uncover something obsolete
some stone formed body
a few pressure-crushed fragments
destined to be cobbled together
into a guesswork construct
just so mankind can pretend
they've found the whole monster
earned the right to name me

I MISTOOK THE WORLD FOR GENTLE

the same way I once chose a cartoon
from a video store & brought it home

expecting disney but in the first scene a dog
is tortured in a pool by labcoated men

to see how long he will try to swim
& in the last scene that dog & another dog

drown themselves in the ocean because
of freedom. this world is not meant for children

either but I didn't know that at the beach
when the waves begged me under & I tumbled

until I was sand-smoothed as sea glass, green
& worn & eventually plucked from the surf

like a tape from a shelf or a new babe
born howling at her very first departure.

MY FAVORITE JOKES
ARE ALL ON GIRLS

my favorite person at the dinner party is the man who boldly assumes I care about fantasy novels. my favorite anxiety is social. my favorite end of the pool is deep. my favorite topic is books-I've-never-read-before. my favorite example is the dresden files. my favorite performance is when he scans the room to ensure everyone sees him loudly acknowledge *jim butcher's female characters are very poorly developed, but the series is a fun read anyway.* my favorite fave is problematic. my favorite praise is a general murmur of approval. my favorite sound is a falling tree. my favorite aspect of this conversation is how it's happening at me but there's no invitation for me to join it. my favorite thing to be at a party is brave, so I say *my favorite fantasy series is the magicians.* my favorite thing about favorites is that each one is a valid point of entry. my favorite sentence is what he says next: *the magicians is the twilight of fantasy.* my favorite part of school is the dismissal. my favorite hammer is a gavel. my favorite literary device is irony. my favorite man-made structure is a wall. my favorite gatekeeper is some dude I've never met before. my favorite heroes are fictional. my favorite genre is the response poem. my favorite color is blood. my favorite conversation is the one I should know to exit sooner. my favorite contradiction in *the magicians is the twilight of fantasy* is that twilight is, itself, a fantasy series. my favorite thing about twilight is that it made a lot of girls happy. my favorite thing about me is I used to be a girl. my favorite thing about men is sometimes they tell me who they really are. my favorite assumption is that twilight is shorthand for laughable. my favorite thing to do is laugh. my favorite way to act is nice. my favorite size to be is small. my favorite face to make is smile.

ODE TO ALL MY MIDDLE SCHOOL CRUSHES

I sleep with the window open like I used to
when *love* was called *like* and Ricky Martin
and the Gin Blossoms still played on the radio
I remember each crush by temperature alone

this specific chill on my nose for the time we
        traded sweaters in a bedroom with canted walls
        hers maybe yellow   mine periwinkle stripe

this precise gust breathing ice on my hair
        for the anxious boy stepping all over
        my best sneakers during *truly madly deeply*

this familiar wind   old friend playing scales
        up my collarbone   for the electric proximity
        of merely handing over a stubby pencil in math

praise this window opening to what once was
my favorite part of being alive: dreaming *what if!*
I think crushes should be called something
more buoyant   more ticklish & lovely

what's the word for falling asleep under heavy blankets
and just at the last moment of unraveling sense
on your upper lip lands a single kiss of snow?

FERVOR

a golden shovel with lyrics from All Star, by Smash Mouth

I spend a lot of time puzzling over memory for somebody
who purports to be unsentimental. but I was once
a child who was so anxious about perception I told
my classmates that my parents wouldn't let me
order chocolate milk at snack time. but the
truth was my mom and dad didn't give a world-
class damn what kind of milk I drank. chocolate is
tasty, therefore it's sinful. no belief in god, so who is gonna
make me order skim? I ordered skim, because. I started roll-
ing my eyes back in 3rd grade. compulsively. picture me
sitting in class, the pressure building until I
flick my eyes and wipe clean the slate. nervous tics ain't
cute. I had another one my mother named the
spasmodic frog. it was a throat thing. the sharpest
words are so often a thoughtless, clever tool.
it's never just one thing that was wrong. in
3rd grade, it was also the year Marty died. the
class went on without him. I don't remember shed-
ding tears. I remember another girl, though. she
wept at the assembly. she howled. I was
too busy feeling guilty to cry, occupied with looking
around, figuring out how one was supposed to look kind.
I couldn't handle memorizing the multiplication tables. of
course a lot of kids have this experience; dumb
because of math. I know now to reject the concept with
a quick, radical fervor. fuck smartness and all. her
scores are the best in the class finger-
pointing status-y nonsense. back then it was what I had and
I clung to *smart* like a castaway clinging to her
life-preserver. I developed a callused thumb
from taking optional standardized tests, filling in
little bubbles that would let me know the
measure of my intellect. or whatever. the shape
I made because everything in me was made of
wrong, tainted stuff. I was sure I was an

awful person. I took it for granted. L-
ook, I don't think there was some overlying issue on
top of my general anxiety. maybe my mother was intense, her
depression residing in our household, scoring forehead
creases of anxiety into my face in my teens. well-
ness wasn't really talked of. but still I think there wasn't The
Trauma that would make sense. I've spent years
trying to figure out what made me start
twitching, loving the wrong people, stopped me from coming
out as queer 'til I was basically 30. and
I don't think I'll ever know. they
never tell you this about poetry. they don't
say it's not real, don't announce Stop
Introspecting, you're not going to be coming
up with anything new or interesting. poems fed
me. poems about childhood. figuring out how to
say this was me, and this was the
peculiar way I moved around. I had these strict rules
about what I could wear and eat and
who I could talk to. never shopkeepers. I
couldn't wear sleeveless shirts, or hit
the pavement in flip flops. the
rule against flip flops was a strict ground
rule. I was concerned I would have to start running
away from someone for my life and I didn't
want to trip. and never fruit. texture. it might make
me sound crazy, but I think it makes sense
if you frame it like survival. like I might die, not
that I was in danger. but maybe my stressed self had to
write my poetry in precaution. I had to live
much like I do now, but these days, for
the most part, I have control over how I have fun.
nobody is telling me hey! pack your
bags and get on this bus with your anxious brain
and all these kids you don't know. it gets
easier when you aren't made to go to music camp. *smart*
is fine. *relaxed shoulders* is much better. but

I don't want it to sound like I was only miserable. your
impression must be: sad. and yes, my head
was so anxious I didn't know it ever gets
better. which is ridiculous, but kids are dumb
self-centered little creatures so
of course I didn't know better. much
later I would fall in love, the reciprocal to-
getherness that good marriages make. but do
you have any idea how much I wanted to be loved? so
much that I thought of almost nothing else. so much
I lied to my private journal about wanting to
have a boyfriend. I didn't want even a diary to see
that I wanted something I didn't have. so
maybe it comes down to weakness. what's
desire besides vulnerability? now, what's wrong
with having an unreciprocated crush? with
being human? kids don't like other kid's human. taking
away the lunchbox to peek inside your family. the
soft fur on the unshaven back
of your legs. I grew up on rural streets
without names and numbers. you'll
see the ocean before you see my house, never
mind the cruelty of children. I know
I'm lucky. I know how it sounds if
I go around bellyaching to you
about what happened in the locker room. don't
think for a minute I'm about to go
around pretending I wasn't just as mean. you'll
need to hear about the poem I never
should have shared. no matter what shine
I put on this story, how it was only wrong if
I knew I had the power to hurt feelings, etc, you
wouldn't buy it. I wrote a don't-
fucking-write-a-poem-like-that poem. I glow
hot when I think about it. 9th grade, hey
whatever, I didn't know then what I now
know about power. about satire. you're

wondering what happened. I wrote an
awful ten-page poem, about all
my friends and teachers, star-
ry eyed and looking for attention. get
it? I got suspended. and more. your
apology was served blushing. game
over. marginally ostracized. transfer schools. on-
ward. etc. so what I mean to say is, go
ahead and call me a bully. it was the rough kind of play
and I've been on both ends. hey,
is your brain also broken? what does it mean, now,
in the context of therapy and ramen noodles to say you're
still broken? what is it about a
little kid with few friends but a tree and a big rock
to talk to that led me here, from a star
pupil to a happy messy person who might get
out of bed sometimes before 9. the
kind of person who will want to show
another poet, beloved friend, how much she is holding on
her back today. I don't know what my baggage is. I get
it for a second sometimes, paid
for in words written, what it means to be a human. and
to have been a child once. have all
of it gone without the hope of knowing that
it was for something. about something. *glitters*
is just another way to say *shattered*. is
just another appendage to dip in gold,
because what else is there to do with a memory? it's only
milk. nobody cares except for me. we're shooting
rubber bands at each other all recess long. the stars
are out tonight, little specks to break
me into contingent parts. each memory the
plaster, every poem as a mold.

THE KISS COUNTS AS QUEER EVEN THOUGH WE WERE PRETENDING TO BE DOGS AT THE TIME

because I said so & because childhood happens on the reverse of the moon
& what is gayer than the moon says I & I grew up wanting to breathe air
and/or underwater yet I never bothered to look really look-look you know
at all the stars I mean opportunities I mean whatever is the opposite of jellyfish
dehydrating on the beach & so when your life is wrapping up will you have
named every kiss after the first one or will you forget to count that one at all
like I know it happened-happened but I also know sometimes people only get to
hold hands in a dream you both have at the same time & if you kiss enough
girls you turn into a planet & I only kissed three so call me Nix or don't call me
anything & I guess the point was I was having puppies & I also know the point
was actually the kissing & it was only a game but if a kiss isn't play do I want it

GROW (IN LBS)

0	
5	first sunlight and screaming tiny
10	fists then milk warm summer
15	light familiar skin sleep arm
20	creases so much milk muscular
25	cheeks at some point banana
30	at some point cheerios pink
35	striped pajamas I see there
40	are bugs in the lawn
45	sometimes slugs on the driveway
50	I am dressed for the
55	very first day of school
60	purple lunchbox colored pencils monarch
65	butterflies scholastic bookfairs snowsuits invariably
70	firetruck red zipping up the
75	front read on the floor
80	of the public library best
85	friends move away hot lunch
90	pizza cold lunch sandwich thick
95	slices of cheddar on white
100	with turkey pepperidge farm cookies
105	the first time I hear
110	a doctor mention my BMI
115	I am asked to play
120	soccer change clothes in the
125	public restroom stall before tennis
130	lessons lift my shirt to
135	look in the mirror sideways
140	frontwise I dream of a
145	sweet boyfriend and start running
150	high school classes I fall
155	in love with a muffin
160	every day of freshman year
165	that fresh lemon poppyseed warm
170	yellow cake flesh throw up
175	I'm a bad kid with

180	a good muffin I learn
185	how to conduct my self-
190	hate quietly off at college
195	I can still shop straight
200	sizes I say that's it
205	I won't be big anymore
210	bipolar lamictal abilify mcdonalds breakfast
215	rum and coke then screwdrivers
220	macaroni and cheese steak quesadillas
225	purge the recession meets me
230	on the other side of
235	graduation unpaid internships I quit
240	purging so I can stop
245	going to group therapy
250	I am asked not to
255	order the chocolate cake at
260	a restaurant but I do
265	it anyway so my boyfriend
270	breaks up with me because
275	I disgust him his words
280	depression lethargy acquisition of a
285	second dog autumn hospital lithium
290	learn how to dress cute
295	for my size stood up
300	for a date at the
305	co-op café deep breaths out
310	becoming a poet the final
315	new boyfriend french fries french
320	fries and love ice cream
325	ice cream and love one
330	percent milk and crispix and
335	love love love I have
340	grown so many good things
345	in this life but loving
350	this body is still hard
355	sometimes I hold my belly

360 and I can almost say
365 nice words she is soft
370 and perfect I can almost
375 say perfect and mean it
380 this morning I surpassed what
385 the scale could weigh of
390 course I'm still ashamed of
395 course of course but there
400 must be even more beyond

- - -

GRIEF : ABSENCE :: PURPOSE :

the ice storm has been teaching me
    how to knit a scarf
        how to start a fire
            how to sit inside
a forest under glass
branches laden   broken arches
the world a museum of itself

analogies were removed
    from the SATs
after being deemed *needlessly*
confusing & irrelevant to success
   I was good   at analogies
the survivor in me asks
        what is success & can I burn it

THIS FLOWERING UPROAR

let us begin / with / the / dance /

after bathing / the peak
of / their / desire /
they move / through the night /

the / mere stomachs, / like, /
breathed / the blessed / oak /
from their mouths /

many / were / dancing / all around
/ their feet / holding / thunder /

all the people look / straight /
as if! /
god / he stands out /
mouth / sweeter than / fresh grief /

remember,
children of / snowy / recesses /
were / always / the /most fearful/

they were like / all / strong / children /
one of them was born / sorrowing in her heart /

children / obey / fear /
all / of them / laughed/

in the revolving years / the sea / began to arise /
grass grew / and / a young girl's / deceits /
stretched with a great recklessness /

sleep and / dreams /
trees / and / destructive / men /

who causes pain / because he is / excessively manly? /
who loves to laugh? / the daughters with beautiful hair /
and / the gorgons / who suffered /
they were, / like, / huge /

there is / they say / an unmanageable thing /
the brutal force of / the / booty /

who / is / a pain?
/ the family /
they are / like / the most / conspicuous /
home is / whoever / is right /

it is good to / be called / beautiful/
who / received / violence? /
who has / parents? /
children / learned / to / swallow / secret / fury /
informed / fat / was / monstrous /
she hid / in / clothes /
put / down /
cruel / and unconcerned /

when / men were / slightly / fat /
the ox / did not / forget /
it / is / living with / bees / all day
something noble / in / rivals /
a great bond / beneath / the / battles /

but / the breasts of them / untouchable /
the unexpected / dread /
the / good things / all of them /
a hundred / heavy / mournful / hands /
all the earth was boiling /
unplowed / and / deprived /
it seemed / terrible /

before they had launched at one another /
they cast shadows /

there is no / being inside the house /
never / look / hated /
he devours whomever he catches /
quarrels arise among / many names /

it is / a great / nine years /
there are / painful /
halls /

sometimes they spoke so god could comprehend /
sometimes they / thundered / and / raged /
tin heated / craftsmen /
blazing / melting / blowing / over the sea /
there is no remedy for this / flowering / uproar /

but, / by / zeus, /
gleaming / and starry /
they / might / be gods

OP-ED FROM THE BALLOON THAT ESCAPED THE TRUNK OF MY MOM'S CAR IN 1989

all balloons should be shaped like balloons / not letters / do not espalier a balloon sentence to a wall / for any reason / even to be inspirational do not do this / it is a cruel abomination / the only message a balloon should introduce is the concept of loft / tension / desire / for elsewhere / & beyond / & before / this is the inherent dignity of a balloon / also do not fill a banquet hall with balloon bouquets / or a living room with mylar minnie mice / do not be cavalier with the balloon / nor take the scarcity of helium for granted / do not photograph a balloon / without her express permission / balloons are the provenance of mystery / specifically childhood / & accumulated dust / never allow a balloon to expire / exhausted on the pantry floor / without proper ceremony / & if you tire of a balloon / do not tell / your beautiful friend / big & yellow & covered in stars / that you do not love her anymore / instead / consider your commitment / a green ribbon tied around your wrist / rekindle what you can / smell that good rubber-skin smell / touch the balloon with the flat of your tongue / please / i urge you / do not let her go

THE CONTEXT OF RAIN

after sam sax

when I say I'm tired of all this shitty weather,
I mean I'm bored by the concept of trauma.
I don't want to talk about casey affleck. I don't
want to pine for sun. once I choked on a piece of steak
but I don't remember the part where I lived.
I can still see the blurring plate, the rough
carved table, scarred steady beast,
the adults all set around it like furniture.
the space between all of them and me.
I must have coughed up the half-chewed meat,
apologetically, dirtying a napkin.
at night I have anxiety about drowning in my own lungs.
my therapist believes there's a good reason
water makes me nervous.
but I think it's just a thing to worry about,
like home invasion or the plague.
comet Shoemaker-Levy 9 dove into Jupiter
on July 16, 1994. the impact was a momentous
scientific occasion—every astronomer knows where
they were when she was swallowed up,
like the challenger or 9/11.
imagine: you need oxygen your whole life or you die.
imagine: being alone inside a planet so big and so red.

& after

HAPPINESS IS OVERRATED

you loved like six men in the same year
and not a single one loved you back.

some seasons you couldn't stop
loving men, your jacket always an evening

jacket, your body a night-time body, you too cool
not to wish yourself into every bed in Brooklyn

but then there was just the you of her,
with your too-thick ponytail and saggy tits

or whatever. sometimes you'd let
your hair down for a date

and none of it had turned white yet.
sometimes men grabbed you by the waist

and you let them do it, too, just to feel
dainty, which was how you defined desire.

sometimes you took baths
and thought about telling your friends

you wanted to kill yourself. your desperation
smelled like windex and yesterday's clove-smoke

clinging to the upholstery.
you bought a glass-topped coffee table,

a subscription to the new york times,
and a white marc jacobs eyelet dress

which said dry clean only
so then you took it to the dry cleaner

because you needed so much
for all the people standing in their perfect ring

chanting *unlove, unlove, the opposite of love*
to be pointing at anyone but you.

SLOW HANDS / DEBASER

the nintendo rented from the video store
comes with one game: duck hunt
I miss every shot (because I am probably four years old)
so I approach on foot
& press the plastic barrel into the television's glossy temple
pow pow pow pow

::

I meet Dan at a Reel Big Fish show in March
but he doesn't talk to me until June
when he and I break up with Becky and Tommy, respectively

Dan acquires my screenname from Jackie
asking me out over AOL instant messenger

we spend the summer driving slow in poorly lit suburban neighborhoods
listening to the one mix cd he burned for me

which is basically just Interpol and The Pixies
music I perceive to be seductive and dangerous
we have sex, once, on the plush carpeted floor of his parents' basement
I am falling in love with July & my car's open window
& all the people I might be someday

in august Dan reunites with Becky
he says: sorry

I am devastated for one week
& then add him to the running tally

PLURALS

I've always liked a good, fancy plural: attorneys general,
poets laureate, captains crunch
I like to google my name to see all the Catherines Weiss—
the mommy blogger, the fine arts model, the civil rights lawyer,
and then there's me, who was once so infatuated with a boy
that freshman year I took a frigid, four-hour bus trip
to hang out and when I knocked on his door he was holding a sign
that said *Welcome Catherine!* decorated with exuberant squiggles
his expression crumpled like slush
sluicing off a windshield, believing he'd been texting
with a different Catherine—another, superior Catherine
I watched both our mistakes
untwist his joy and never have I wanted more
to exchange who I was for somebody else,
to fling open the hatch and say
welcome, Other Catherine, you can take it from here
this is the one we love
he's about to invite you limply inside
and you will stay, of course, unwanted as the clumps of snow
clinging to the bottoms of your pant-legs
later, he will shrug the poster-board into your hands—
do with that whatever you want

DRIVING AROUND MY HOMETOWN

being from a place means having a bleak,
boring story about all of the rite-aids. you become
tour guide for your most rural minutiae.
this rite-aid had the good blank CDs, I used to burn
mixes with an external drive, remember
those? that's the rite-aid he bought the condoms at,
told me to wait in the car—I was too young
to understand why. I always thought one day I'd leave,
I just assumed. this rite-aid got built after
the supermarket burned down. we saw the tower
of smoke, green sky overstaying its evening.
suddenly my whole life is at the front door, fumbling
for missing keys, half-hoping to slip back in.

LOOK HOW MUCH YOU DON'T KEEP BEES

our neighbors have a well-tended garden
with a tall wire fence around to keep out the deer,
a modest greenhouse, and chairs to sit in
and, presumably, bask. they also have beehives—
two white boxes visible from our back door,
which honestly feels like an aggression, like
look how good we are, neighbor, tending these bees.
we, on the other hand, being city folks moved here
from away, have not mowed once all summer
but there is the milkweed by the driveway, so
when pressed I take credit for the monarchs
and the wild lupines by the stream blooming
abrupt purple stalks. when I say we've been
talking about buying a gun, I mean we are trying
to believe there is a soft future waiting for us
and we are failing. once, in Texas, a gun was placed
into my startled hands in my own living room.
it was a dainty little thing, like nettles pulled
from a handbag. I wanted to throw up.
I wanted to puncture the world, watch it spin
around the room defeated. I've heard a forest
cracking under a flood of winter, succumbing
one by one to the bleak pressure of a long Maine
darkness. if only I were the kind of person
who doesn't know what ice does to trees.

THE WINTER CATALOG

A. **Hot Pockets.** Ham and cheese
flavored. Two pack of microwavable
shrug. Always to be prepared and
eaten two-at-a-time. Color: Wet khaki.
Sizes: One size fits all.
L20410. Hot Pockets. $4.

B. **Seasonal Depression.** Wind howl
bluster and waiting. Useless days
spent mostly in bed. Frosty twill, flannel-
lined, if you're lucky. Color: Ice, Gravel.
Sizes: S, M, L.
L20411. Seasonal Depression. $0.

C. **Iron and Wine.** Various songs
but especially that one from Twilight.
Imagine if loving yourself could be
gentle as a melody. Color: Evergreen.
Sizes: XS, S.
L20412. Iron and Wine. $8.

D. **This Dress.** Short-sleeve, mid-calf
length, crew neck. Unwashed but hopeful.
Pockets, hallelujah, pockets. Patient
gifts to our timid selves. Color: Grey.
Sizes: XL, 2X, 3X, 4X
L20413. This Dress. $70.

E. **The Memory of a Fox.** Just
yesterday, a trotting friend in
the dark. Fluffy tail, little feet.
Things to live on. Color: Red-brown.
Sizes: S, M.
L20414. The Memory of a Fox. $0.

BUT ANYWAY, HOW ARE YOU

I seem to be doing this thing lately where I preface
the answer to *how have you been?* by saying
I'm sure this is just the depression talking, but...
before I launch into some overwrought discourse
about bees and ocean acidity and how photosynthesis works
(though I do not know how photosynthesis works)
to lament our dying planet and how humanity is doomed
and then I explain that it occurred to me the other night
after watching too-much netflix that all the art
that's ever been made throughout history will stop having
significance the moment nobody is left alive to argue over it
not the 90s one-hit wonders or the not-read stacks of new yorkers
and I'm pretty sure an unread poem still counts
but I worry an unreadable poem is just a bunch
of molecules that threw a tantrum one time
and then I go on to explain to my visibly horrified
spouse/friend/colleague that I've been spiraling
because the emptiness humankind will leave behind
is already sorrowing the backyard songbirds and
isn't the impending silence just impossibly tragic?? I ask
and then I do the worst thing of all which is laugh
dishonestly at my overwhelming anguish and confusion
before finally blaming this whole outburst on
the obvious target of February with a shrug that
assures everyone my fear is not so large that I can't
tuck it politely into my pocket and get back to work
and it's only much later after I have driven home and had
a good sullen sit and the cheesy half of a burrito
that it even occurs to me any of this might in truth
have actually been the depression talking and it's not
that I'm too cool for hope it's that mental illness
is just something about my body I have gotten used to
like fatness or knee-caps but sometimes there's a sunny
patch of snow over by the fence and I am alone in the kitchen
for a minute neither sad nor un-sad and then I remember
that eventually there may be thaw

56

REDACTED NAMES OF PEOPLE I'VE LOVED AND THE CURRENT DISTANCE BETWEEN OUR HEARTS

[   ] 8 ft
[   ] 6 mi + a clock
[   ] 15 mi
[   ] 154 mi
[   ] 313 mi
[   ] 326 mi
[   ] 532 km + a closed border
[   ] 335 mi + the agreement not to mention it
[   ] 368 mi / a phone call + something interesting to say
[   ] 3278 mi heading east + many things I should have done
[   ] 3347 mi heading west + many things I should have done
[   ] 472 mi + 10 years + many things I shouldn't have but did
[   ] 1235 miles + a hard block on Facebook
[   ] some amount of miles + 20 years + fraying gingham anger
[   ] salt + fear + fear + time
[   ] a hummingbird's wingbeat + 2 big cries + 4 little ones + only 15 oz of regret

THE ONLY TIME I'M NOT IN LOVE IS

i remind niko to draw wheat

he refuses to trade sheep for rocks

we both roll punitive sevens

wood and brick makes a useless road

i do

what i have to do

catan unsoftens me

everyone is tired

this is the difference between us:

he never wants to play

& i want to forgive him

WHEN WE PLAY SETTLERS OF CATAN

we are driving over the bridge

from the island to the mainland

consider the fragility of a supply chain

& other things that could kill you

in sickness & in health

starvation is a bit dramatic

on a tuesday afternoon

i ask: at what point do we consider suicide?

niko says: look, an osprey

niko says: the plan is we stay together

SHE LOST WEIGHT; HE GOT TALLER

once upon a time I lived with a man
who, by the magic that only happens in one's twenties,
became taller whenever I lost weight.
it was an exciting discovery.
he'd always wanted to be tall, I'd always wanted
to be loved. we discovered the spell
when I had the flu, me sweating on the blue
quatrefoil couch, a week of ginger ale;
his pants too short. the arrangement worked
for a while. I was hungry but he was happy.
he touched my belly and fed me greens.
o, how women in bars looked at him
then. *I could have cheated on you tonight
but I didn't,* he'd say stepping long-legged
into bed. how tall must one get
to have a heart attack? I'd wonder,
as I laced up my running shoes.
how small can I make myself today?
yes, I do believe in love.
I drink the stuff like I'm dying of thirst.
what wouldn't you do for a man
who used to kiss your ear? at the toilet bowl
he glanced down at me to say, you're disgusting.
he stretched his arms and took
up the whole house. one night I tried a piece of cake,
dense and good, with chocolate frosting rich as a sunset,
and he told me to stop. so I ate another.
I don't like what's happening to you,
he said but what he meant was
I don't like what's happening to me.
he was shorter. I ate all the sweet things
I could taste and he grew smaller
and smaller. I ate salt, and I ate seconds.
as he diminished, he howled like a let-go
balloon. at last, my body was soft, round,
done; my hunger, too, extinguished.

FOR THE MEN COMMENTING "GORGEOUS" ON MY PHOTOS

some words are not good words, like *moist* or *panties*. I forgot gorgeous clicks my burner right up to high, a kettle calling the pot gorgeous.

if I showed you a picture of my first-loved house, wallpaper licked clean off after fire, after fire, after after, would you call the shot gorgeous?

I know. I knowww. I'm tedious but I'm also *butterface. butterface. butterface. butterface. butterface. but your tits are hot, gorgeous.*

there are the men I want to want me, abstract flames. there are men who smell like men I knew before I was angry, before I got gorgeous.

I wanna be wanted from afar, specifically. stand at canyon's lip and fill me with your pitiful echoes. this is how you court gorges.

you can call me anything; brave or good, kind or Catherine. call me awful taunting names. fat bitch. fat ugly bitch. I'm not gorgeous.

NOTHING TASTES AS GOOD AS BEING NOTHING

the respected psychiatrist
assumes I've always been fat
he thinks I'm only *like this*
cuz I've never known the joy
of texting men
angular collarbone selfies
I tell him

        I used to be thin

he licks his lips
pen poised
takes my history in lbs

hard   it seems
is this man's favorite type of data

he will meet me only once
so this department head doesn't know
I learned the thrill of pressing my flat belly against
boys in basements and men in bars
how the sweetness of body
burned my tongue young

doesn't know how many
filled me up with their desire
left me wanting less

the psychiatrist puts down his pen
   pleased
      as if he's solved a challenging sudoku

when he tells me I wouldn't be depressed if I lost weight
what I hear worming its way through his words
is the belief that if men as a societal unit
might want to fuck me
at least I'd have something to live for

62

NEW YORK CITY, 2005

you know how sometimes your boyfriend's name is Mark
& his roommate is a cop named Marc   but with a c

& you pretend like that's a super funny story
& you pretend like being alone with them
                        does not make your skin crawl
& you pretend like you agree borrowing
        real handcuffs for sex is totally hot
until Mark shows you how much it isn't

Mark is seeing his ex behind your back
he thinks you don't know because you don't say anything
            he & you are now facebook official
                    Mark being tall, cheekbones chiseled
you are so compatible he says
                you are learning compatibility is compromise
                plus a man doing what he wants

you know how sometimes your boyfriend uses certain words
            and you ask him   maybe   not to

he thinks it's funny
            and what can you do except freeze the smile
when the only person laughing
                holds the keys you need to leave

EVERYTIME WE TOUCH, CASCADA, 2006

the man who works behind the counter has a crush
on me. he and I are alone here and
I take pleasure in warmly ignoring him. I read
an actual book with turnable pages. maybe
something by Jonathan Safran Foer.
I linger over infinite refills of diet coke.
I'm probably hungover, depressed,
avoiding homework. definitely wishing an
inappropriate man would text me back.
I come to this cafe almost every day this year.
somehow, there is only one song that ever plays.
funny how passing time pulls memory inside out.
balls it up. tucks it softly in in a drawer.
this memory, a confection. mille-feuille. past it,
a knitted sweater. spider's web. tide-pool.
reach in to find my empty hand

WHERE I WENT, OCTOBER 2012

Once I dreamed there were three men from different histories and they rode horses together into the future. Once I dreamed Donald and Barron were trying to hang out with me at the beach and I said no. Once I dreamed I was crawling through a lake of my own hot blood. Under my house is a mineshaft. A rusty world—quiet, dirty. Sometimes I dream about taking the LIRR to the city. The change in Jamaica is always across a field and sometimes the trains have no walls. I have a recurring dream about a mall where every store has clothing that fits me. I dream about taking the escalator to the top of the Saks Fifth Avenue mountain. I dream about a food court parking lot. My therapist two therapists ago. A house with a back staircase. Going again to boarding school, all grown up. Walking reverse into the ocean. Divorcing my husband by accident. A boat. A dock. The moon, too close. Subterranean cafeterias. 14th street. Bodegas. I don't dream about the psych ward. Not ever. No locked doors or placemat menus. No ping-pong in the hallway. No showers before dawn. No charging my phone at the nurse's station turned sideways. No linoleum floors or hanging ceilings tiles twisted into caricature. It was too simple, maybe. Too boring a story. Once I spent a month leaving my city while locked inside of it. Once I called it my city. And then I disappeared.

I CAN'T TELL IF I'M OK IN REAL LIFE BUT SUPPOSEDLY ALL THE CHARACTERS IN MY DREAMS ARE PLAYED BY ME

so I look for my face in the shopkeeper's face,
find myself in the taffeta wall beyond
her back. fifty champagne dresses
hung up to the ceiling and I can't decide
which face to wear to prom. here I am
in my old city's face, a park dribbling
down its center aisle, cigarette tracks
smoking east to Montauk. I'm in my grandfather
clock's face. I'm in my trickster ocean's face.
I'm dressed in my finest mother's
mother's mother's face. here's my face
as the earth's face, as seen from a jewel
toned vacation, my face shattered into rainbow
spectacle by all these comets with my dimple.
my face, here's my face as a grown
boy's face. he turns to me from the window,
showing me our forlorn, pink wet cheeks.
he already knows why, tear-formed stalactites
stretching out as if to kiss.

CONFINEMENT

in captivity once
a beluga whale
learned
to mimic a human
voice
pitch & rhythm
they thought she
said "get out"
so the keeper
climbed out of the tank
whale   was
done with
hearing only her
desperate
solitary thoughts
reflected from
a concrete wall   belugas
are captured
because they are expressive
&
they die less often than
other whales in
confinement   but water is
not enough
to keep being
alive   she knew how
to grin big
look happy
no one
understanding   she wanted
not to die
in this cage

I took a shower
in the dark
& brushed teeth
put on clean clothes
applied
make up   in the psych ward
somehow
I do all the right things
in return
the doctors say I'm
certainly
improving   they
say I look
like I am
employed
in the hospital   this is because I am
on vacation
at a daycare
for the mentally ill
if I worked
here   I would be
even more
visibly depressed   it's just
I wish they knew
my illness is
frightening
but if I called them all
assholes they'd
give me
more drugs
& force me to talk
of myself

NOBODY CARES ABOUT MY DREAMS UNTIL I ADMIT WE FUCK IN SOME OF THEM

we trade dicks at the end of the world. a mushroom cloud unfurls
on the horizon. waves lap at the second floor of my childhood home.
a tumbling moon. we press mouths in the cellar. sometimes you are
the most beautiful person I've ever seen. sometimes you are a washcloth.
we touch in ways I'm not supposed to want. a warm, radioactive breeze.
I can feel it coming now. swelling up with the tide. soon. the conclusion.

ARS POETICA

"See, the secret to a kiss is to go ninety
percent of the way, and then hold."
- Will Smith, "Hitch" (2005)

I have dreams where people
who are not supposed to touch me

touch me. They put hands on
my face, breasts, between my legs.

They wear baby pink lace collars
while I skim a new yorker article

by or about a man who wanted
to die and then did, gladly,

through some vanguard
bureaucratic apparatus

to make there be fewer americans.
How much am I going to give you?

How much were you planning to take?
I am not now nor have I ever been

a crabapple tree,
but I would like to kiss one,

maybe, on a bluff surrounded
by gold grass.

I wait, tiptoe
amongst the fallen fruits—

inedible rot, made soft
with understanding.

LESSONS LEARNED BY WATCHING ONLY THE FIRST HALF OF BOOGIE NIGHTS

career prospects are rosy if you're a white guy with a giant knob

if you're stupid yet charming your friends will ~~be nice~~ profit

cocaine has never gotten anybody in serious trouble

that's probably Julianne Moore's secret kid calling the party

but I'll never find out

because if you are willing to stop watching then any movie can end happy

this does not work in real life even though I wish it did

I turned off *The Road* after they found the bunker full of canned food

I turned off *Titanic* after the sex scene even though that boat already sank

my future grief is a cruel body of water my house sits right next to

all the birds in the universe are telling me to turn off my TV

before it gets worse and I know everybody is going to be so so nice

to that Mark Wahlberg doofus until it's his time to be a tragic figure

I just want to feel fine but sometimes there's a river

and nothing is humane

HOW TO MAKE A FILM FESTIVAL

bricks are made out of heat and clay.
carrots are made out of water and sunlight.
roads are made out of asphalt or dirt or gravel
or sometimes cobblestones too I guess.
thoughts are made of invisible anchors
tied to invisible kites. lies are thoughts
with tangled-up strings; dreams are coins
made of fog made of breath made of sleep.
when I try to go to bed I remember
how once I said I would start my own film festival.
I said this to many people (including my boss
who already ran a film festival) who now all know
I failed. any plan is comprised of equal parts
dreams, thoughts, and lies. sometimes I think
I am furniture—even my sorrows are mediocre.
did you know, some people are made of mulch
and shame, like how a tree believes it is made
out of tree until it is already the coffee table.
if you ask me, the future is made up of erosion—
the daily subtractions of grief from time.
a proliferation of back-buckling frost-heaves
in the pavement, the way made impassable
by the arrival of yet another temperate spring.

ASSAULT SEEN FROM AROUND THE CORNER

using only words from the first page of American Psycho by Bret Easton Ellis

the guy, calm,

has red on, maybe.

someone young and alone at the wall.

I'm thinking

of my fourth or my seventh. what

is the price of living with an all-

American fear?

this is not a dirty movie.

the fact is we're an asset

for the unscrupulous. I hate

society

and the alternative

cannot afford me.

no. enough. not

another. don't abandon hope

all ye who give a shit.

I told on him, Baby,

I care about you so.

EYELET

once I donned a white eyelet dress & rode the L train
    to Morgan or Montrose, to give an artist a hand job.

in exchange, he painted my portrait, oil on canvas.
    I sat on his futon & drank his wine, considering his

industrial loft, his half-dozen roommates, his coveralls
    dabbed in cream. the artist asked me to stay the night

& I considered that too, turning his offer in my unwashed
    palms. a magpie muse with her silver coin. when the

paint was dry, I took myself & left. joyfully, precisely,
    I nestled our painting in the trash.

ALL GEESE ARE SAD

don't make generalizations about geese.
you don't speak goose.
you can't solve goose problems.

eventually the lone gander honking panicked circles
through a murky sky falls silent.
refuses to crack the night with calls

for his missing wedge.
this goose
is not ok.

you want so much to help.
I see you.
aching to shoot it down so you can nurse it better.

but geese don't need you.
you can only watch
from the ground as they live a life apart.

both of you desperate.
both of you halved.
naked feathered ghosts.

PAIN

the pain in your left breast has taken
on all kinds of significance since you knuckled
under and made the doctor's appointment.

driving to the bank you think: this is what
will kill me, this here cancer of the left breast.

having lunch you think: I must not tell anyone
how much I am looking forward to writing
urgent poems about mortality.

driving to therapy you think: what will happen
to my facebook profile? driving away from therapy
you think: what will happen to my husband?

by the time you arrive at the waiting room you are
already bored of having cancer of the left breast.
you are ready for the next thing to happen.

the doctor palpates your tissue and it hurts
more than you expect. you have forgotten you did
not also invent the pain in your eagerness to die.

it's a muscle strain, says your doctor, kindly.
she must think you are reassured by the news.

she must think you are

   somehow
      here

          in this room
            at all.

RECOVERY INSTRUCTIONS FOR PEOPLE WHO NEVER FINISH WHAT THEY START

a found poem consisting entirely of first steps from random wikihow articles

sit down / choose the moment your readers will enter the story / reel in the fish til you can grab it with your hand / don't lose control / use a blade for straight cuts / understand the cost / write out how alcohol affects you / limit your consumption of certain painkillers / remove any hazardous items from your home / respect that horses are powerful and complex animals / be sure this is what you want / practice in front of a mirror / check for mood disorders / learn to recognize pheasants / separate the egg / look for blood / consider what you might need / choose the right rope / seek medical help / remove your jetski from the water / think back / look for a stinger in the wound area / don't let it define you / find a comedic angle to everything / harvest the lavender before it's fully in bloom / wash your face / give it some time / set your ego aside / decide on your message / start with nice friends / pour out all the nectar / take recommended medications / find a clean sock / set up a dance space / let the wax dry completely / ripen the mango in a paper bag / ascend slowly / prepare to be daring

SUGAR & PORNOGRAPHY

the first step to recovery
is admitting you have a problem

        somebody scientifically established
        that birds dream about singing

the step before the first step to recovery is googling
"porn addiction" in an incognito browser window

        a dream happens inside a parenthesis
        like a finger touching its own knee

I quit the pills when I get lost on the way
to the bathroom & pee on the floor

        when I say I dream about the ocean I mean
        I dream about where the water flirts with the land

I don't drink for a year & I miss the harbor
its tongue tide, wet rippling beach jaw cove

        in my dreams I taste desire sweetly
        so in my dreams I must still be 12 years old

it's sobriety if you don't count the shopping
& gossip & sugar & pornography

        a bird's dream song is a dress rehearsal so
        he can perform without a wrong note

what should I quit
to become a happy person

        what if it's happened many times
        & each morning I forget

what if I dream my first step every night
and someday I'll wake up just knowing

                    how to sing it perfectly
                    all the way to the end

UPON RETURNING THE U-HAUL ON TIME, WITHOUT CRASHING

I'm the kind
of person who can't
cook because I won't hold
sharp objects. my hands
inevitably shake
and then I overthink it:
maybe I am the kind of
person who pushes
a blade to my thumb just to
be dramatic about
forgotten tomatoes.
and yet! I have successfully
navigated this cargo van
through several towns
and also in reverse.
someone smoked in there,
apologized the guy
handing me the keys.
I tried really hard
to get it out.
I've conquered
parking lots, driven in rain.
I am the kind of person for
whom renting a u-haul
and returning us both
intact is an accomplishment,
but not once have I mistaken
a pedestrian for a plastic bag
or a red light for a moon gone
hungry. I am doing it all correctly,
become the kind of person who says
yeah, I can drive a u-haul,
knowing it is cruel and also true.
I want to stop in the middle
of this intersection

and nap in all the unused
furniture pads. I want
to drive to a new town
and buy a house
without bringing any boxes.
I want extraction from all
the things I said
I was capable of doing.
I drive on king street,
past the stop & shop
and liquors 44. through the
green light turning yellow,
grasping the wheel with
skeleton hands, windshield
wipers playing on the radio.
strangely, I am not done
doing these things
I don't want to do, thank god,
I am still as here as the smoke
inside these tired
cushion seats.

WE PLAYED A GAME OF WOULD YOU RATHER

in bed last night I asked my husband
if he would rather live in this world as it is
or in a world without suffering
but humans had never evolved
the concept of humor.

he was quite distressed.
laughing is the whole point of being alive.
he said it like a question.

I understood what he meant though,
and we were quiet for some time,
probably both weighing
the occasion we guffawed til our stomachs
hurt due to a very lewd joke we made
at Jimmy Stewart's expense

against War, Unspecified. Genocide,
Unspecified. Cruelty, Unspecified.

how featherlight all jokes
then seemed. how expensive
and ill-conceived.

though I don't think I would have fallen in love
with my husband if all we had
to offer were observations
of each other's facts, like cats or owls.

and I'd miss Jimmy, too,
his folksy awshucks ways—

or maybe just our unkind impressions
of him that kept me
alright all winter. for a moment the memory
is almost enough to be relieved that our world is cruel
in all the ways our world is cruel.

THIS IS WHERE I WILL UNBECOME

yesterday someone was pissed at me
so today I am moving to Maine
to live in an old farmhouse
on a hilltop surrounded by blueberry barrens.

my house will have seven bedrooms
and only one bathroom.
it will smell like wreathmaking
and bread dough rising in yellow bowls.

the only light allowed will be of mid-September
afternoons—motes syruped into a stately waltz
which I'll conduct from the kitchen window
with a wooden spoon.

I'll let the grass grow knee-high
and there'll be lupines and clover
lined up the gravel driveway.
I will wave to them whenever I pass

like the queen. behind the house will hunch
a crabapple tree and a snarl of wildflower
I will call my garden. of course, in Maine
I won't be afraid of all the bees.

and there will hang a clothesline, obviously,
three posts painted green, gray rope
smiling them together. this time,
bedsheets exhaling into somebody else's memory.

sometimes I want to tell you what happened
without telling you what I have done.

ACKNOWLEDGEMENTS

Some of the poems in this book were previously published in the following journals, sometimes in different forms. Big thank yous to their editors for supporting my work.

"all geese are sad," *I Can Count to 10*

"but anyway, how are you," *The Mantle*

"confinement," *Noble/Gas Quarterly*

"the context of rain," *Counterclock*

"eyelet," *Sybil*

"this flowering uproar," *Tinderbox Poetry*

"for the boy who might have loved the ghost of me," *Up the Staircase Quarterly*

"for the men commenting 'gorgeous' on my photos," *petrichor*

"grow (in lbs)," *The Mantle*

"how to make a film festival," *Up the Staircase Quarterly*

"I can guess what instrument you played in middle school band," *petrichor*

"I can't tell if I'm ok in real life...,' *The Shore*

"lessons learned watching only the first half of Boogie Nights," *Freezeray*

"look how much you don't keep bees," *Fugue*

"my favorite jokes are all on girls," *Meat for Tea*

"new york city, 2005," *Voicemail Poems*, as Model 3.5

"nonbinosaurus rex," *The Mantle*

"nothing tastes as good as being nothing," *Eunoia Review*, as Dr. Worm pain, *Noble/Gas Quarterly*

"redacted names of people I've loved and the current distance between our hearts," *Birdcoat*

"Sorry Day," *Hobart After Dark*

"sugar & pornography," *petrichor*

"the kiss counts as queer even though we were pretending to be dogs at the time," *perhappened*

"this is where I will unbecome," *What Are Birds? Journal*

"upon returning the u-haul on-time, without crashing," *The Shore*

"where I went, October 2012," *Birdcoat*

"why am I like this," *The Mantle*, as "I think I know more about the world than I used to"

A version of the poem "fervor" was first published as a chapbook by Ginger Bug Press.

NOTES

"before the harvest" is a pantoum

"wolf girls vs. horse girls" is a contrapuntal

"for the boy who might have loved the ghost of me" is a sestina

"fervor" is a golden shovel, a form invented by Terrance Hayes, using lyrics from All Star, by Smash Mouth

"grow (in lbs)" is an invented form with five words on every line

"this flowering uproar" is an erasure of Hesiod's Theogony using text from the translation by Willian Blake Tyrrell

"the context of rain" is after a poem called "poem about water" by sam sax in Bury It (Wesleyan University Press, 2018)

the title of "happiness is overrated" is borrowed from the title of a song by the band Airborne Toxic Event

the title "slow hands / debaser" is borrowed from the titles of songs by Interpol and The Pixies, respectively

"the only time I'm not in love is when we play settlers of catan" is a contrapuntal

"for the men commenting 'gorgeous' on my photos" is a ghazal

"confinement" is a contrapuntal

"assault seen from around the corner" uses only words from the first page of American Psycho by Bret Easton Ellis

"recovery instructions for people who never finish what they start" is a found poem consisting entirely of first steps from random wikihow articles

For the myriad combinations of friendship, mentorship, support, and inspiration, I want to express immense gratitude to Robbie Dunning, Jasmin Roberts, Jelal Huyler, Kay Dymek, Huimin Wan, Cori Stenning-Barnes, Matt Bayne, Michael Medeiros, Tara Bernier, Kai Pretto, Lauren Singer, Adam Grabowski, Madeline Lessing, Sam Capradae, Jay Deshpande, Megan McDermott, Zeke Russell, Alex Woolner, Jason Montgomery, Lewis Morris, Devin Devine, Wheeler Light, Taylor Steele, John-Francis Quiñonez, Lip Manegio, Sam Rush, Jess Rizkallah, Jonathan Martel, Ewan Hill, Simone Beaubien, Blue Nguyen, Morgan Ureña, Lyd Havens, Jason Koo, Eloisa Amezcua, and CA Conrad. High fives and hugs to Josh Savory and the Game Over Books team for believing in this work. Endless thanks to my family. Most of all, thank you to Niko, who makes everything possible.

FEB 5 1993

ove wolves. I
think wolves are
byuttyful.

Catherine Weiss is a poet and artist from Maine. Their poetry has
been published in Tinderbox, Up the Staircase, Fugue, Okay Donkey,
perhappened, Birdcoat, Bodega, petrichor, and Counterclock. Catherine
was the 2017 Grand Slam Champion of Northampton Poetry and has
competed at the National Poetry Slam, Women of the World Poetry Slam,
and Individual World Poetry Slam. They illustrated the interactive poetry
chapbook and deck of cards, I Wish I Wasn't Royalty, also from Game Over
Books. More at www.catherineweiss.com.